Given Time
A Mother-Daughter Cancer Memoir

poems by

Christine Beck

Finishing Line Press
Georgetown, Kentucky

Given Time
A Mother-Daughter Cancer Memoir

for
Miriam K. Beck
10/10/27 – 1/9/78

Copyright © 2025 by Christine Beck
ISBN 979-8-89990-027-3 First Edition
All rights reserved under International and Pan-American Copyright Conventions. No part of this book may be reproduced in any manner whatsoever without written permission from the publisher, except in the case of brief quotations embodied in critical articles and reviews.

ACKNOWLEDGMENTS

The following poems were printed in *Blinding Light*, Grayson Books, sometimes with different titles: "Aftermath," "What Goes When Flesh Goes," "To the Core," "Lining the Casket," "Given Salt, Given Time," and "What I Never Wanted"

"Spirit Masks" originally appeared in *Connecticut River Review*

Publisher: Leah Huete de Maines
Editor: Christen Kincaid
Cover Art: Van Gogh, Olive Grove at Saint-Remy. Gothenburg Museum of Art, Gothenburg, Sweden; Courtesy of Wikimedia Commons
Author Photo: Marvyl Garnier
Cover Design: Elizabeth Maines McCleavy

Order online: www.finishinglinepress.com
also available on amazon.com

Author inquiries and mail orders:
Finishing Line Press
PO Box 1626
Georgetown, Kentucky 40324
USA

Contents

Part I

Outside the Frame 1
Aftermath 2
To the Core 3
Given Salt, Given Time 4
Hair 6
Lining the Casket 7
Spirit Masks 8
You Can't Have It All 10
Begging Bowl 11
What's Inside 12
What I Never Wanted 13
Refrigerator 14

Part II

Between the Lines 17
First 18
Diagnosis 19
Waiting 20
Linked By Strands of Pink 21
Predicting What's Ahead 22
Sutures 24
Feeling Good 25
Before I Knew 27
What Goes When Flesh Goes? 28
Tattoos 29
Congratulations 30
Bequest 31
A Year Goes By 32

Foreword

As the years go by—it's now forty-seven—since my mother died of breast cancer, I find myself growing closer to her spirit. That is only partly because I was diagnosed with breast cancer in 2023. It's not really our cancer connection that compels me to reach to grasp her hand, to recall our trips to Europe, or listening to Jean-Pierre Rampal's flute, or canoeing on Lake Carnegie in Princeton. It's not just how I've bestowed my mother's love on my three adult daughters and my two lively and loving granddaughters.

It's the recognition that we all offer gifts to those we love. Some we recognize at the time if we're lucky. Some we don't see until we are far apart.

The title and cover are based on a trip my mother and I took to Spain, after my mother's cancer had recurred. We ate black olives and drank white wine on the beach. Black olives take time and processing to be edible. I like that image because it knits together our lives—the juicy joy of eating olives, waiting for the cancer to progress, enjoying life full throttle, and the processing of grief.

My mother and I live in these pages as the vibrant spirits we were and continue to be.

Part I

Outside the Frame

We are framed by wild roses,
wearing mother-daughter dresses
my mother made.

Green apples sway on white piqué.
We squint into the sun, sandaled, tan,
in wait for some forgotten fete.

My mother could turn tissues
into pink carnations,
dole out charm like Cheerios spill
into a breakfast bowl.

I wear her smile, catch her infectious
laugh, her love of brilliant clothes,
embrace the thorns hidden
just beneath the blooms.

Aftermath

While I was sashaying down Telegraph Avenue,
hips swinging, syncopated to the Rolling Stones,
breasts bobbing beneath my leather jacket,

my mother had been lying on a metal gurney,
clammy to the touch, lips gray, not knowing
she'd awake to find herself one-sided.

I fly home. She wants me there to witness
the unveiling of her bandage. The scar
runs like a ragged river across her chest.

Soon pills line up like tiny foreign coins.
They buy us seven years, while in her desk
she's hidden notes marked "*Funeral Instructions.*"

To the Core

The lilies on the sill spread a soporific scent,
yet you lie awake, ponder in the dreadful
dead of night.

Your left breast amputated, after months
of biopsies, second opinions,
indecision.

What goes when flesh goes,
the firm freshness
of invincibility?

What would you be if you were peeled away
to just an apple's core—no shining ruddy skin,
no pungent flesh exuding golden juice,

just a toughened stem, pale yellow,
a handful of black, shining seeds,
keepers of a buried truth?

Given Salt, Given Time

I.

Before I knew that olives grew in Spain
and bloomed on ancient trees,
their accent on the tongue of foreign zest—
kalamátas, arbequiñas, manzañillas,

Before I knew that olives should grow full,
turn black or purple-brown on branches first,
then cured in brine for weeks in wooden casks,
their bitter taste stripped out by salt and time,

I thought black olives came in cans called *Ripe*,
displayed on crystal plates in Large or Jumbo size,
unaware they'd been picked green, then dunked
in lye and gassed to turn them black.

II.

Before I knew what burrowed in her skin
would claim my mother's life, wrest it away,
leach out exuberance, her gift of flair,
strip hair from blonde to driftwood gray,

We holidayed in Spain, slipped into bars,
bought local wine, a meal with cheese and bread,
where *aceitunas*, olives, were required
to turn the commonplace to the sublime.

We feasted on their oily olive skins,
their soft resistance, ooze against the tooth.
With flick of tongue against each fingertip,
we licked the dripping oils and sighed.

III.

That was before I knew what I knew now,
that olives on the branch, grown full and lush
will lose their clutch. They fall into the nets
below, still bitter and inedible,

but soaked in brine and stored in casks,
given salt and given time, the olives turn
as delicate as memory, as piquant
as a picnic on a small Majorcan beach.

Hair

How do we always know,
the scarf tied just so. Underneath,
a pate, smooth as buried bones.

No give, no squeeze or swirl,
no wisp escapes to curl
into a question or a promise.

Like dandelions when the petals
dry to husk, pearlescent emissaries
sent by wind to burrow into dust.

Splayed against her pillow,
two-inch strands of what was gold, now
gray as gritty snow, weeks without shampoo.

Will she live to see it sprout
like baby fuzz, then grow into a pixie
cut we say is *just the cutest—so easy.*
Look, we say, *how easy it will be.*

But ease has gone. It packed its bags
when they abandoned chemo. Ease lives
in the land of *Pat the Bunny.*

Lining the Casket

Two are black and white, feisty, thirsty; the third,
soft yellow, like sunshine mixed with baby carrots,
we name Calico, a patchwork guinea pig.

It's the runt, a slip of fur and darting eyes, skinny
as an anorexic, heart pounding through her fur. My daughter
loves it with a passion reserved for the unlucky.

Its mother runs away when Calico approaches.
I take the healthy babies out to force what can't be forced.
I briefly think of killing it, then recall my father's tears

when he tied kittens in a sack and drowned them.
I tell Calico, "You can go now," then feel a fool
for playing hospice with a guinea pig.

I didn't say goodbye that January night, when my mother,
wrapped in cancer's iron fist, stopped asking if the sky was blue.
I took the train back to Manhattan, to the job she bragged about.

I recall the flowered dresses with matching panties
she smocked for me, as I line a cardboard box with chintz,
head down the hill to meet my daughter at the bus.

Spirit Masks

The leader brought the clay, instructed us
to lie back, apply it to our faces,
tear breath holes for nose and mouth,

> *What spirit in gray clay,*
> *the feel of pitted city sidewalks,*
> *smelling like a wet retriever?*

eye holes too, although opening my eyes
seemed risky with the grit.

> *Is spirit conscious, playful*
> *like a child gasping at the apex*
> *of a roller coaster, breathless for the plunge?*

Each mask unique, she says,
recognizable as a Polaroid.

> *Or downcast, like the eyes of penitents*
> *at Scala Sancta, marble steps worn thin*
> *through centuries of crawling on their knees.*

We stripped them off, laid them in a circle,
walked slowly searching for our faces
in ghastly grimaces like Edvard Munch's "Scream,"

> *Is spirit eternal? My mother's,*
> *buried beneath the dogwood,*
> *her ashes the color of these masks?*

The message of the masks obscure,
like a fetus with fins before
fingers start to spread.

> *Does spirit travel to the past, keep memory*
> *alive, or does it hurtle forward, caught*
> *in black holes beyond the natural world?*

De-spirited, my spirit skitters out,
seeks release from this forlorn mask,
an empty shell of clay.

You Can't Have It All
after Barbara Ras

You can have the first crocus of spring
huddled in the undergrowth. You can have the rabbit
that pops up from its hole, its purple velvet eyes aglow.

You can have the late afternoon sun inching
between leaves of evergreen, casting
an amber glow, last gasp before night befalls.

You can have your books, the ragged and the lost,
the ones you can't forget, the doppelgängers
and the dwarves, hunger artists, human bugs.

You can't have your mother back, your trips
to European castles, her laughter like a jazzy flute,
a thermos of martinis, her chocolate mousse.

But you can have her words—in letters, recipes,
address books—words that flit like fish in a brook.
Scoop them up, untangle them from hooks,

smooth out the lines, release the grief
      of everything unsaid.
            You can have that.

Begging Bowl

After the news that she would die.
After the bargaining: *take me, take me.*
After the cruelty of unearned pain—
    What then of comfort?
    What of hope?

After I had introduced myself to grief,
After screens and tests, prognosis,
After I had made a mask of cheer—
    What then of comfort?
    What of hope?

Fill this gaping bowl with just enough to live today.
Force out my fear, scum at the bottom. Lift it
up to overflow the rim. Let our connection—
the cord that bound us without words—
    Let this be comfort.
    Let this be hope.

What's Inside

My mother's wallet, worn red leather. I've moved it from drawer
to drawer these forty years since she's been dead,
as if one day she'd show up at my door

headed for the grocery, needing the coupons tucked inside,
as if she'd need my brother's photo
in his goofy glasses, back when he had hair,

as if she craved a whiff of leather, before plastic
took its place. She'd gauge its bright red heft, back when
twenty bucks could see her through a week.

I've bought and tossed ten wallets since she's been gone,
photos of my kids replaced by licenses, credit cards,
twenty bucks now grown to hundreds.

Still, today I crave what's in this wallet,
I open it, shake it inside out,
hoping for a coupon for a double bonus life.

What I Never Wanted

Ashes in a vase, September mourning,
distant calls of loons, a fractured sky,

sullen earth mounded under dogwood,
leaves burned hot as afterthoughts,

afternoon of unbelief, wall of windowpanes,
hangers in the closet, askew and bare,

fragile chattering, a sound like empty acorns,
dried nutmeats, the harvest passed.

Refrigerator

I

It speaks inside,
the jumble of bottles,

boxes, shrink-wrapped,
half-opened and expired.

The yogurt growing
a slim sheen of slime,

the cheese sprouting
spots of mold, like craters

on a silver moon,
its evanescence slowly

settling like a bottle
of half-drunk beer.

II

It speaks outside, jumbled
on its door, clipped by magnets,
yellowed tape, the menus,
photos, random calling cards
of workmen, those who seek
to fix the crumbling structures,
unclog the pipes, get the motor running,
fill up the empty cauldrons.

III

It speaks in a wild confabulation
of snap shots from the past—
the moment when:

> we first learned—
> we booked the trip—
> we paddled our canoe,

as if the lake would rest as crystalline and calm
as we felt on that summer day, you in your crooked
sun hat, matching smile, me lifting high the paddle.

IV

It speaks of hungers satisfied,
that can never be satisfied,
of meals for one, or none.

Part II

Between the Lines
    A cento of lines from Part I

Laughter like a jazzy flute
    A picnic on a small Majorcan beach

Witness the unveiling
    Smooth as buried bones

If you were peeled away
    Embrace the tiny thorns

Given salt, given time
    The commonplace becomes sublime

Slowly searching for my face
    Green apples sway on white piqué

Pills like tiny foreign coins
    Shining seeds, keepers of a buried truth

Dried nutmeats, the harvest passed
    Down to the core

Buried beneath the dogwood
    What I never wanted

You can't have it back
    Fill this gaping begging bowl

I didn't say goodbye
    Two-inch wisps of what was gold

Smooth out the lines, release the grief
    Of everything unsaid.

First

First take his hand and place it gently on your breast,
that is, the hand of the Archangel Raphael,
which you would not do if he were flesh and blood,
but as he is an angel and as no one is looking,
perhaps you'll take a chance.

First decide which archangel is the one for healing.
No, not Michael. No, not Gabriel with all his tidings,
those good tidings, which you haven't heard in quite a while.

First meet the surgeon with her perky plastic clogs,
her sympathetic eyes above her face mask,
watch her draw you pictures of where she plans to slice.

First decipher the pathology report with words
you can't imagine ever knowing or wanting to know,
how they string together in a sequence that seems to be a story
with no plot, no characters, the ending impossible to fathom.

First place your breast in a vise,
hold your breath as your breast is cinched in pain.
Say it doesn't hurt. Lie and say it doesn't hurt.

First disrobe in a dressing room with an accordion folding door,
cheerful posters on the wall. Find a paper gown,
tie it in the back, no, in the front, no, it doesn't really matter
where you tie it, it won't be tied for long.

First answer the condolence cards: thank you thank you thank you.

First, bury your mother.

Diagnosis

She is so young, this doctor, so full
of facts, theories, diagrams to remove
the tumor, restore me to myself.

In her white coat and Covid mask,
she asks to see my list of questions,
as if she's prepping for a test.

Yes, I'm grateful that it's highly treatable.
Yes, I'm glad she can fit me in her schedule
for surgery next week.

But I don't want to feel grateful.
I want to clasp hands with my mother,
dead over forty years of this same cancer.

I want to feel the softness of our befores,
the innocence of tomorrows without fear
of what lurks beneath our skin.

Waiting
    by Rebecca Bryan

Like the geese in the sky
I like to move with the wind
Always knowing where I'm going.
Even if the aviator in me says *turn this way or that*,
I stay the course of my path.

The pain doesn't dissuade me.
The distractions don't win out.

      But this cancer, it threw me off balance.

Of course, it did.
It didn't mean to do this to me.
I don't take it personally.
I know I'll find right side up again.

Still, bear with me.
I'm dizzy sometimes,
turning upside down.
Waiting.

Linked by Strands of Pink

Like tree roots stretch, seek each other
beneath the earth, lie dormant, then link
to support the seedlings as they emerge,

when it appears the stump is dead,
smoothed by weather and the years,
its rings grown faint and indecipherable,

our roots lay quiescent in the years
since you've been dead, no shoots,
no hint of green, tendrils linked by memory

of laughter, travel to foreign cities,
kittens in the baskets, our fashioning of flowered
sundresses, picnics with martinis in thermos bottles.

Then a link we had dismissed, a link
like an unexpected shoot, composed
of cells and vessels, long underground.

We are linked by strands of pink,
the blood that coursed through
your veins and then through mine.

The doctors say I'm just unlucky—
no reason to think my diagnosis
is related to yours forty years before.

But I know that like I learned from you
to carry yarn beneath my knitting, to hold
the strand waiting to link up with a swan

or heart, waiting, holding on with proper
tension—not too tight, not too loose—
I know we're linked by strands of pink.

Predicting What's Ahead

My grandpa was a farmer,
dependent on crops and livestock

for his livelihood.
Years of squinting at the horizon

for a hint of rain, or worrying
the snow drifts would delay

getting to the milking parlor
were embedded in his DNA.

He read *The Farmer's Almanac*,
a guide to the coming year—

weather forecasts coupled
with homespun advice every farmer

had already figured out.
Farmers must be crafty to outwit

the uncontrollable, depend
on an unknown future.

Did he believe it? Any of it?
Or was it just a reminder of how hard

he worked to work the land
and keep his spirits up?

Perhaps *The Farmer's Almanac*
is as reliable a predictor

of my future as this BRCA test,
a sequence of my DNA, hazy lines

that could portend a tornado
on the horizon, or maybe one
that won't arrive for months to come.

Sutures

At twelve, I was a dress form for a jockey,
as my mother sewed his *silks* in royal blue and gold.

A man about my size would wear this shirt
as he raced around the track, his compact

torso snapping like a riding whip, shirt
and jodhpurs soaked with mud and sweat.

Snip. Sew. Turn inside out. Even up the edges.

I held my breath against the prick of pins, my body
still as a thoroughbred before the starting shot.

Royal blue and gold, regal winner colors.
Bold   bright   invincible.

French seams, resistant to the pull, strain,
muscles tensed for a race against time.

Snip. Sew. Turn inside out. Even up the edges.

Feeling Good

The way the sun extends its tendrils in the dawn
can make you feel like you are heading for the airport
for an early flight to Tuscany.

Hurtling down the highway to be sure
you won't miss your flight. You feel eager,
until you glance at the papers

lying inert in your lap: Hartford Hospital,
surgery at 7 am. A destination as far
removed from Tuscany as a tractor from

a pin cushion, which is what you are about
to become, as you slide your arms
into a hospital gown festooned with faded flowers,

as an IV line is inserted in your arm,
and you are just another passenger waiting
for the operating theater where they ask

what kind of music you'd like to listen to,
and you say Michael Bublé's *Feeling Good*,
although you hear only a snippet

before the anesthesia takes effect.
Supplanted by the hum of fluorescent lights.
Slice of scalpel through flesh.

You wonder where you were while the surgeons
hovered over you. Where did your spirit go,
not in the land of dreams, not in Tuscany?

Were you inert like those instructions, lying
under lights bright as Tuscan sun? You swim
up from the darkness, where even dreams

are banished, where time stood still.
You wonder if you are feeling good,
if you will be feeling good next year in Italy.

Before I Knew

Before I knew what I know now,
I thought I had escaped, I thought
the dark angel had passed me by,
as if I'd sprinkled blood above my door.

Before I knew what I know now,
I thought the years of broccoli, brisk walks,
no alcohol and yearly mammograms
offered me assurance.

Before I knew what I know now,
I thought my mother's death was grief
enough to fill my begging bowl.

I didn't know that dread can creep into a crevice,
spread its fingers like a child scoops out a lick
of peanut butter, hoping to evade detection.

Before I knew what I know now,
I thought a minor surgery, a bit of flesh removed,
would heal with such an insubstantial scar,
I wouldn't notice what was gone.

But now I know that scars remain,
that pain will come at unexpected times,
like a rainstorm on a tropic island, a sudden deluge
unleashed from what I thought were clear blue skies.

What Goes When Flesh Goes?

It measured millimeters, not enough
to be deforming, breast an awkward slant
where a robust melon used to be.

But it was flesh—mine.
Was it cut out and tossed
in a bucket called "human waste?"

How does the word lumpectomy
translate to missing flesh?

What goes when flesh goes—
the firm freshness of invincibility?

Two years ago, tall pines presided
over my deck, dropped pinecones
from thirty feet to loam below.

Then they were chopped down.
They weren't diseased.

Experts said their roots had burrowed
near a rock wall, could crack
and crash what seemed invincible.

No second opinion for tree surgery.
Were trunk and branches
treated respectfully as living matter?

How to preserve the imprint
of my good years and bad,
like rings on bare stumps
of those missing trees?

Tattoos

*I want for what I love
to go on living,* Pablo Neruda

Between my breasts, three tattoos
the size of pinheads mark the spots
to guide the radiation's beam.

No artistry, not like lines from Neruda,
that weave up arms of those who seek
inspiration to seep into their skin.

My friend designed her own tattoos–
three bees on her ankle for her three sons.
Then three intersecting circles on her arm.

My three dots don't form a picture.
A child could not connect them
to reveal a kitten or a turtle.

As I'm lined up on the metal gurney,
I think of my three daughters,
grown, but not yet old enough

when mammograms will mark
their calendars with dark-inked
spots of dread.

Congratulations

"Congratulations," they say, at the end
of twenty days of radiation.

"Congratulations. You're done."
But what is done, you wonder,

Your skin brittled bright red, the shadow of
the metal eye rolled back into its lair.

No cake, balloons, no goody bags,
just two white-suited technicians

who scan their sheet for the next woman
who will enter, wrest her arms

out of her faded johnny, expose her flesh
to flashing red lights, the slight hum

that signals radiation, as she holds
her breath for twenty seconds to force

her lungs to shield her heart.
How can you shield your heart?

No way to judge success,
no test to take, no imaging

to reveal a negative. Just wait.
Deflated, like a birthday balloon

loses its lift, drifts despondent to
the floor, deflated in the aftermath

of what was once a celebration.
"Congratulations," they say.

Bequest

I bequeath to you, the scent of apples
on the trees in the back pasture,

the bees that swarm the fallen fruit,
the juice that seeps into the earth.

I bequeath to you the color of the evening sky,
the dip and swirl of starlings, alighting

for the night, their screech and chatter
as they rustle into rest.

I bequeath you too my half empty perfume bottles,
the memories of where and when each scent

lingered on my skin, became as much my signature
as pen and ink on pale blue parchment.

Also, my pen collection, the ones exhausted
of their usefulness, the ones with zest to grapple

with an empty page, the words they wrote
that mingled with the ones they haven't met.

I bequeath you these: my soul's embrace,
my signature in scent and rhyme,

the apples printed on my childhood dress
of white piqué, its sway in evening's breeze.

A Year Goes By

This year the leaves have fallen
in a rush, as if the ground were paradise,

as if they didn't know they'd be swept up,
bundled into paper bags and burned.

I can't unpack my bag. It lies on my bed,
contents dirty/not dirty. I lack the energy

to sort them out, the bright thoughts from the dark,
the whiff of lived in from the never worn.

I long to soar above the clouds, emerge
into a clarity that shocks. Where is that blue,

a blue that pulses like a vein beneath silken skin
as white as alabaster?

I am made of molecules, like those leaves, intersected
with lines from stem to tip, like the elms and oaks,

jumbled together before they break apart,
meld into a substance soft as ash.

My body feels substantial, as if it could hold the weight
of memory, words left unsaid. But words grow heavy,

like survival tools packed in a backpack,
unbearable as the miles mount up.

The future beckons with ancient fingers.
It has no crystal ball, no deck of cards, no way

to predict if next winter I will feel delight
in a first snowfall or the despair of endless gray.

My face is a map of these twelve months,
lined like autumn leaves. It bears the aftermath

of last year's jaunty piles of clustered colors,
and those pale brown bags, waiting to be filled.

Christine Beck holds an MFA in poetry from Southern Connecticut State University and is the author of three books of poetry—*Blinding Light* (Grayson Books 2013), *I'm Dating Myself,* (Dancing Girl Press 2015) and *Stirred, Not Shaken* (Five Oaks Press 2016). She is a former Poet Laureate of the Town of West Hartford, CT. and former President of The Connecticut Poetry Society, where she created a poetry series called Poets on Poetry.

She has also written *Beneath the Steps: A Writing Guide for 12-Step Recovery* and leads workshops for writers in recovery.

She publishes a weekly essay about literature and life called "Beck and Call" at *christinebeck.substack.com*

Her website is *www.ChristineBeck.net*

www.ingramcontent.com/pod-product-compliance
Lightning Source LLC
Chambersburg PA
CBHW020220090426
42734CB00008B/1148